JOY SHARED

Joy Shared

Solee MacIsaac

EVERY BOOK PRESS

MMXXII

© Copyright 2022 Solee MacIsaac
All rights reserved.
ISBN: 978-0-9837714-4-9

Book Design by William Bentley

TO THE READER

These thoughts were written from February to July 2021. They include daily experiences from home cloistering and short trips to the West Coast of Northern California. Each day represents a musing slice of my inner and outer life. It gives me pleasure to share with you a silent and hopefully enriching journey together. Please read slowly and let the images cover you with joy.

Solee MacIsaac

This little book is dedicated to all of my friends and family with whom I have shared joy; and especially to my husband, Robert.

Page after page,
Word after word,
Heart speaks to heart.

February

    Sparkling drops on tree trunks,
Wet pine needles,
      Melting light.

    Cat gaze,
Rain-glazed window,
      Gray longing.

    Light of the world
Speaks.
      All is alive.

Tangled branches
Greeting dawn
With sleepy shake.

Moss-covered tree
Sheltering horse
Munching grass.

Radiant threads,
Small spider
Weaves sunlight.

Curled oak leaf
Cradles
    Caterpillar.

    Striped circle
Of cat,
    Ears twitching.

    Whisper,
Night dreams,
    Craving to wake.

Through vaulted clouds
Redeemer shoots
    Love beams.

Interlacing
Bare branches,
    White sky, snow?

Trip to West Coast

    Dew kissing
New blades
    Shimmering green.

    White clouds
Huddling
    Blue mountaintop.

    Gleaming flecks
Celebrating
    River's bend.

   Endless traveling water,
Ocean's body
   Rife with gulls.

   Lathered ocean skin
Erupts
   Sea lion.

   White sea meshes with sky.
No beginning,
   No ending.

Hummingbird
Wildly attacks
      Swaying heliotrope.

    Sweet river
Meets salt ocean,
      All tears forgiven.

    Sleeping dragon
Pretending
      To be a hill.

        White spray
Whipping
        Black rocks.

        River mouth
Kisses
        Ocean crests.

        Light stretching like taffy,
Touching eyelids,
        Snapping back.

Egret, black cows,
Wild mustard,
      Fluorescent grass.

    Drops of living water,
Lily mouths
      Open wide.

    Valentine's smile
Redly plump
      To bursting.

White mounds
Softly breathing,
　　Sleeping lover.

Trip across California

    Early morning cloud
Nestled
    Between two trees.

    Velvet green landscape
Sprouting vineyards.
    Wine country.

    Misty Sonoma hills
Hiding
    Black grape vines.

Home

    Summer dreaming,
Shivering,
    Beneath heavy blanket.

    Looking up
Wishing,
    You and stars.

    Boundless milky arch,
Quietness
    Invades my soul.

Ears tingling,
Piano trills,
        Climbing skyward.

    Sad tree shares
Bending boughs
        And heavy leaves.

    Light on light,
Innerly
        Blazing awareness.

      Grace curves
Around
         Sweetest smiles.

      Greatness belies
Size,
         Modesty every time.

      All is light,
Even the darkest corner
         Crackles.

Digging for truth,
Deep nuggets,
    Shining gold.

    Umbrella of light
Scattering
    Night dreams.

    World-weary cat
Plods valiantly
    To his bowl.

Gray dawn,
Sleepy shuffle,
Starting breakfast.

Inside and outside,
Eyes in two directions,
See vast landscapes.

Aging slows down
While everything else
Speeds up.

Long road,
Shimmering trees,
    Speaking Spring.

Light spaces,
Infinite, timeless,
    Stretching true.

Thoughts like flies,
Who are they
    To me?

Piercing global silence
Small cat
　　　Wants out.

　　　Thick white soundproofing
Covers town,
　　　Coldly quiet.

　　　Remorse sings
Sadly
　　　Through inward eyes.

Inside out,
Then
        Outside in.

    The Real
Exists as unreal,
        Really.

    Selfish delusion
Covers
        Empty heart.

        Trees whispering
Questions.
        Wind answering.

        Eye light,
Knowing,
        Tickling laughter.

        Sky lights,
Streaming,
        Eyes watering.

Before creation
One speck
      Illuminates all.

    Sand, waves, birds
Swinging
      With sea song.

    Resting simple,
Lasting quiet,
      Oceans of blankets.

Counting clouds,
Do they look the same
From above?

Inner smiles,
Walking through
Limitless memories.

Bacon sizzling,
Toast popping,
Breakfast pleasures.

Spring hints
Climbing over
        Windowsills.

    Boundary between
Sea and air
        Shimmers in sunlight.

    Dainty drops
Quickening cadence,
        Turns to roar.

Green on green
Spring
    Returns alight.

Green teepee
Of vines and branches
    Safely shelters sprout.

Wind winds
Round the house
    And catches its tail.

This is a haiku.
A hidden meaning reveals
   True simplicity.

Digging in the soft earth,
Worm wriggles
   In my rough glove.

Last day of the month,
Last opportunity,
   Still Sun shines.

Mountain speaks to lake
In hushed tones,
    Coaxing duration.

March

    Bursting bulbs
Grant their bounty
      With nodding yellow heads.

    Green, black, blue and white,
Colors of early Spring
      Pulsing into eyesight.

    String of islands
Dot the blue ocean,
      Sending a green message.

Morning grumbles,
Coffee, tea, toast.
World looks better.

Voice in my head
Turns me around,
Keeps me confused.

Light breeze
Lifts my hair,
Sun warming every strand.

Golden air
Buzzing with life
        Above grassy pond.

        Cavernous echoes
Defining space.
        Internal emptiness.

      All creatures
Run, fly, swim, crawl.
        Vines climb to God.

Ducks in a row.
Interested cat.
Yellow feathers drifting.

Numbers infinite
Pointing possible
Pathway to Eternity.

Amid multifaceted
Life patterns,
Awareness point captured.

Moss-covered rocks
Draped with new leaves.
      Willow blessing.

    Vivid contrast between
Sunlight and shadow.
      Moving leaves flashing.

    Cat warmed by
Fireplace,
      Stretching languidly.

Big soft white flakes
Melting on everything,
    Coldly beautiful.

Drops chase each other
Across the windscreen,
    Eye focus shifting.

Cream cheese clouds,
Sapphire sky,
    Greenest hillside ever.

Waking rest,
Silence
        Inside and out.

    Laws form
Archetypes,
        Puppets frolic.

    Lavender fields,
Aroma rises,
        Orifices open.

Inside out umbrella,
Snow catcher
    Supreme.

Sun sun sun,
Eye opens,
    Brilliant.

Sprinkling of yellow heads,
Cool green river
    Slithers darkly.

Shoreline shells,
Toe crunching
      Wet mystery.

    Large lacy flakes
Land on my hand,
      Melting slowly.

    Mystified kitten,
Ice crystals sting
      Under small feet.

Earth labors under
Heavy rains,
    Blossoms explode.

Bird palettes
Yield melody,
    Spring sings!

Honey bees
Carry sweet nectar
Home.

Moaning winds
Chase memories
    Into hidden crevasses.

    Eagle pierces wild blue sky,
Splitting
    Heaven from Earth.

    Cold hands,
Foggy yard,
    Hours stretching.

Hiding behind daffodils,
Pretending to be
A bee.

Dragons descending,
Streaks of color,
Sun sets again.

Fireplace crackles,
Cat in a bag,
Diners have left.

March is long,
Summer beckons,
      Up periscope.

    Grateful hands
Smooth the way
      To glad giving.

    Dangerous side-glances,
Those blue eyes,
      Wink too many times.

A rose or two
Or three or four
   Opens every door.

Grace bestowed
On lighted crown
   Clears vision.

Angry violence
Puzzles
   Mind, heart, and soul.

Goodness spreads
Evenly over
    Big glossy cake.

    Rain-drenched white horse
Munching
    Green glowing grass.

    Nerve endings of
Empty wet branches
    Go sky reaching.

Mozart, green tea,
Smiles and toast.
New day begins.

Heavy sky,
Moist earth,
Long lasting quiet.

Rain begins,
Dotting roof,
Hypnotizing cat.

Piano chimes lightly,
Violin joins,
      Soothing all woes.

    High-definition light
Picks out
      Every dark secret.

    Inner silence,
Outer peace,
      Tranquil day.

Reach up,
Reach down,
    Pull the ends together.

Radiating pulses,
Sounds aligning,
    Patterns emerge.

Lavender fields
Fragrant and warm,
    Bees, birds, and song.

Sunlight
Streaming through the blinds.
    Time to go outdoors.

    Spherical shallow world.
Going deeper,
    Rotten core.

    Snails and turtles are slow.
How fast would you go,
    Carrying your house with you?

        Places in the world
Call out
        To my traveling psyche.

        Dinner with friends,
Heaven
        In the earthly realm.

        Throw the dice.
Whatever numbers appear,
        Count your blessings.

Trapped on Earth
Watching soaring birds:
       Are they watching me?

    Wondering about
Space,
       Is there really any?

    Sweet clover growing
From soft moist earth
       Between my toes.

New growth,
Vines climbing,
 More space, more light.

Trees out my window
Are shouting
 Spring!

April

April blinks,
Sunlight floods
 Every crevice.

Ladders raining all around,
First step
 Is all it takes.

Simple moth
Flutters too close
 To curious kitty.

The world is fair
But not just.
    All creatures endure.

Love soothes wounds,
Love holds dear,
    Love encircles life.

Grand is the day
When I can see
    My true self shine.

Open the windows,
Open the doors,
        All is forgiven.

    Rejoice every day
You can love,
        Open hearts bleed less.

    Thirds, fifths, octaves,
The harmonic universe
        Sings life.

Witness your moments,
They are ephemeral
And eternal.

Attention focus
Is a treasure.
Spend wisely.

Rare is the being
Who has courage
To look deep inside.

Sun transforms the night
Into day.
        Find your inner sun.

    Ever optimistic
Bird song,
        Springtime melody.

    Good luck isn't lucky,
It's appreciation
        For whatever transpires.

Shadows stretch across
The late afternoon,
Boding nightfall.

The world is vast and varied,
But only a drop
In the ocean of the universe.

Feet touch the ground
Lightly in joy,
Heavily in woe.

An umbrella of light
Changes sight
And insight.

The bones and flesh of Earth
Don Mardi Gras robes
Every Spring.

Our heart's center
Is an ever moving
Circulation of light.

Dip your cup
In the fount of pure joy,
    And be love-quenched reborn.

Ripe fruit hangs heavy
On the branch.
    Pick carefully.

Do I have something to say?
Or,
    Do I have to say something?

Listening to the silence
The volume
    Hurts my ears.

    Is it still news
If you don't want to know it,
    Or tragic voyeurism?

    Having you in it
Makes a house
    A home.

Growth and progress
Are not the same
    Steps to increase.

Work is play
In the right
    Frame of mind.

Clean your house,
Spring blossoms
    Can't sit on dust.

Laughing dragons
Line the path
    To Eternity.

    Swans on pond
White grace
    In many ripples.

    Water lily leaf,
Green platform,
    Frog respite.

Asleep, awake,
Earthly cycles
　　Blinking in and out of existence.

A grand gesture
Dwarfs a helping hand,
　　But the hands know.

Morning light
Stirs the breeze
　　Atop the sleepy willow.

Count the many
Cloudlets marching
       To Earth's cadence.

    Third time's a charm,
But first and second
       Can cause alarm.

    Personal interest is an illusion,
One for all
       Is closer to the truth.

Granite, iron, diamond
Are not as firm
As inner determination.

Focus attention,
Focus intention,
And surrender to love.

Each step marks
Another opportunity
To re-see your direction.

Joyful sharing
Spirals up
    In all who partake.

    Racing through morning air,
Tires humming,
    Road winding upwards.

    Dancing sun sparkles
On water's edge,
    Cat drinks her fill.

Out of time
Things slow down,
    Stopping has no meaning.

    Time to eat,
Time to sleep,
    Time to see the clock is me.

    Dark eyes,
Heavy lids,
    Sleep approaches again.

What is mine?
Except responsibility,
All else belongs to Gods.

Dainty drops
Blowing in the wind,
Land on my eyelashes.

Clarity depends
On the inner eye,
The rest is just vision.

You wake up one morning
And wonder,
 Who is in the mirror?

The space in my head is large
When the competing voices
 Stop.

Words tumble forth.
What is behind?
 Is there meaning?

Grandiose plans,
Grace comes
      Moment by moment.

    New meaning
To a labor of love,
      Love comes first.

    Trees don't complain
About having to
      Produce fruit.

    Sun outshines other stars,
Closeness
    Can obscure the real.

    Rocking to the lullaby,
Babies remember
    Life before birth.

    Music speaks
A language
    All understand.

Complex thoughts
Expressed simply
    Is intelligence.

    Celebrate your life,
Each being adds
    To the grand symphony.

    Small tasks
Loom large
    Procrastinated.

Sweetly vibrating,
Beauty, Music, Love.
   Higher harmonies.

Feeling strong,
Spreading goodwill,
   Two-way happy.

Making plans is fun,
Following them,
   Easy to deviate.

Watching kitten
Learning patience
    And precision.

    Gravity is a jealous lover
Coveting everything,
    Breaking free is enormous.

    Hot coffee brewing
Fills the morning air
    With bright promise.

Another birthday,
Another gathering,
　　Sweet friends rejoice.

Generous with time,
Unaware
　　The little remaining.

Green days slide into
Burned hay-colored
　　Summer months.

Laughing, crying,
Feelings expressed,
        Waste deeper perceptions.

    Accepting difficult moments
Can lead to
        Healing understandings.

    Moments are not really
Difficult,
        It is in us – the difficulty.

Watching me,
Watching you,
Watching.

Counting the money
Doesn't make it
Worth more.

Impatience signifies
An unhappy
Soul.

Lavish decor
Cannot uplift
    An unclean space.

    Good conversation
Can replenish
    All parties' spirits.

    Oceans of mystery
Cannot deviate
    A constant heart.

A witnessed error
Can spark
    Fiery conviction.

A curious mind
Can learn lessons
    Through experience.

Smallest roses
Make a nosegay
    For eyes and noses.

Sweeping landscape
Nourishes
    A sleepy mind.

    Reach out,
Touch the tips
    Of resting mountains.

    Temperate, moderate,
Sage, wise, and tolerant
    Cradles the gestating.

All monsters vanquished.
Under bed space clear.
Earned rest appreciated.

April finishes with rain,
May splashes in
With every fragrant blossom.

Clear skies,
Moist earth,
Lovely Spring morning.

Cats jumping and playing
In new sunlight.
Green grass abounds.

Dragging my feet
Walking behind,
Pokey-Jo follows the rest.

Slow and careful,
Taking in everything I can,
Open to the wondrous world.

Open minds can connect,
Fearless and loving,
    Offering many insights.

We love each other
To the depth
    We can reach in ourselves.

If I think I know everything,
How will I learn
    Anything at all?

May

    May Day peeks out
From April's cloak,
      Raining petals.

    Traveling beacons,
Temperate days
      Slide into fragrant nights.

    Waking with the Sun,
Light rays inside and out
      Reveal sleepy thoughts.

Go with me
Through my day,
    Bring clarity to my sight.

Only you can open
Doors inside and out,
    Cherishing every moment.

Changes can upset
Or release new energy,
    If we are not stiff-necked.

Lavender cool
Petals on smooth pond
Obscure reflections.

Streaming shafts of sunlight
Choose the privileged
To enhance in gold.

Waking birds in trees
Sing the glory
Of wondrous morning.

Darkness flees before
Shining heroes
    Rebuilding the world.

Made of conviction
A fortress
    Crumbles from necessity.

Lost in fantasy,
World goes on.
    Can I catch up?

Missing moments,
Bitter taste,
    Reminding to pay attention.

    Remember to be grateful
Each time
    The rug is pulled.

    If there is no change,
There is no time, no growth,
    No progress, no love.

To evolve,
The spiral up
Is a rigorous climb.

The difficulty, the effort,
The reward
Are one.

Ancient messages
Support
Relentless aim.

How fast
The days stream by
        In endless cycle.

    Is the world really old,
Or only
        Me.

    The body machinery
Continues.
        Who runs it?

        Living water
Falling
        On thirsty ground.

        Cool light of intelligence
Warms in radiant
        Pure bliss.

        Overthink
Reigns atop
        Decaying mountain.

Green dragon
Hovers over
    Silent white lily.

    What gift
Is better given
    Than received?

    How much would cost
Most precious gift?
    Who can receive it?

Wandering through the forest
Trees speak to me.
   Listening is hardest.

Cat fight,
Sounds scary,
   Winner preens.

Lucky are the ones
Who perceive truth
   Through love.

Gratitude surpasses
Brilliance, glorious success,
　Or even modesty.

　School lessons seem tedious,
But learning
　Opens all the windows.

　Tropical island
Orchids, bananas,
　Endless beaches, volcano.

Frizzy curls,
Sapphire eyes,
Singing throat of gold.

Simmering
Beneath the surface,
Ideas spring forth.

Not everything is worthwhile,
High value,
Difficult to come by.

Glissando up and down,
Many notes do not
        A melody make.

    It's okay to love everyone
Just don't
        Add any strings.

    Strawberry muffins,
Spring delight,
        Bake smoothly.

Mothers cherish,
Provide, let go,
    Then repeat.

Always tomorrow,
Never today,
    Childhood lament.

Banners, balloons,
Celebrating
    Merry-go-rounders.

Oakey wine,
  Smoked cheese,
      Picnic party.

    Flying fingers
  Only skimming keys,
      Gorgeous sound ensues.

    Who loves a thing
  Gives it meaning
      And its own beauty.

Angel mine
Are you mine?
    Or am I yours?

Spider hanging in midair
Waiting
    For dinner to arrive.

Our lives are little packets
Divided by planet rotations
    And cycles round the Sun.

Recurrent motions
Giving credence
    To earthly forms.

    Words in a row,
Letters following a sequence,
    Where does meaning arise?

    Communication
Between writer and reader
    Is silent and intimate.

Beauty lives and breathes,
Sweet light surrounds
Such earthly glory.

All eyes sweep to such
Perfection,
Heart and mind genuflect.

A feather slipping through
Air currents
Lightly lands on my hand.

Cotton ball clouds
Rolling across mountain tops,
    Trees bending to roiling pond.

    Nature placid, Nature bold,
Her two faces
    Smiling wide.

    Soft steps barely heard,
He returns.
    My lover is beloved.

Grand and lavish
Summer struts forward
Making the scene.

Animals have their lives
In the envelope of earthiness
Barely touching humanity.

Hearts endure
Long nights of dark places
Patiently waiting for sunrise.

Greeting dawn with new eyes,
Laying down old woes,
Picking up a mantle of hope.

To graze the fields
And feel the sun,
How does a cow thrive?

Old cat moans for dinner,
Young cat scampers
In sunlight.

Centuries pass.
Those who come after,
Who are they?

Existence flees
Before the tide of time.
Backwash carries us out.

Summer sun blazes
Shriveling grasses.
Fire spotters nervous.

Natural world,
Shy and bold,
      Keeps us sane.

    When are we
Fully grown
      Inside?

    Feelings erupt,
Minds intend,
      Bodies follow.

Actors, musicians, painters
Are all vehicles to convey
Higher energies.

To be a conduit of art
Is a blessing.
The craft is hard-won.

Magnets are a mystery,
No matter how much
Explained.

So much of the world
Exists
    Someplace else.

    Meatballs and gravy
Kind of day.
    Smells good.

    Orchids grace
Hearts and eyes
    A very generous time.

The space womb
Creates the Earth pearl
   To rotate in magnetic bliss.

Oblivious to our fate,
We shoulder on
   Into the darkest night.

Dawn wisdom shines
Upon foreheads
   Of only grateful accolades.

Ancient times living with
The same fears and joys.
        Still have to make the bed.

    Dessert seems superfluous
Until it is
        Taken away.

    Disturbing sleep,
The angel grasps
        My hand again.

How can I justify sleep?
Sun rises every day,
So must I.

First sip of coffee
Stings lips,
Satisfies nonetheless.

Vibrating, pulsing,
Waves, colors, sounds,
Life is busy.

Antennae raised,
Lightning flashes,
        Renewed direction.

    Strange visage,
Long shadows,
        Avoid despondency.

    Good cooking brings
Warm feelings
        To giver and receiver.

Drizzling gray day.
Hot chocolate and comfort
Coming up.

Serving without heart
Is only mechanical
Motion.

Dancing with myself,
Enjoying the grace
Of fluid movement.

The foot steps lightly
On its way
    Home.

    Clearing inner space
Is more difficult
    Than sweeping the kitchen.

    Even a false alarm
Sends out waves of concern
    To all interconnected.

Light
With no shadows
Is invisible.

Lost in the snow once.
Followed my footprints
In circles.

Gated garden
Emits fragrances,
Luring peeks.

Light from the galaxy edge
Must be tired,
        Such a long journey.

    Milky Way
Stretches wide and narrow,
        Heaven's Riviera.

    Friends come and go,
The world whirls round.
        Stopping, not an option.

Opening and closing,
A fish mouth,
What water?

Climbing higher
Baby rose bush
Seeks more light.

Are rocks compressed earth
Or is earth
Ground up rock?

Don't think about a rock,
It'll make you
    Crazy.

Roses unfurl every petal
To bask
    In the morning sun.

Blossoms open to the sun
Because
    That's what flowers do.

Roadblocks are the norm
For anyone
    Trying to get somewhere.

Trial of body sensations,
Fodder of desires,
    Always a challenge.

Many Me's
Lost in who's first,
    Who's loudest.

A bubble of light
Surrounds this me,
        Growing inwardly.

        Sauerkraut for dinner,
Friendship
        Is dessert.

    The dark inner world
Is lit up
        With two-way awareness.

A drop in the still pond
Engenders endless circles,
    As a spark in a quiet mind.

An image
Tells a story
    In no words.

Lofty crane
Bends to the ground
    Same as the lowly pigeon.

One foot leaps forward,
The other
    Reluctantly slides behind.

    The Word
Sings out,
    All things are manifest.

    Stories enthrall
And instruct
    Minds young and old.

Wind terror, running fire,
Water immersed,
Smoke rise. Fini.

To remain securely firm
Within the sacred space
Is moment-by-moment work.

Many hands
Make light work,
Many 'I's make no work.

Fresh strawberry cream pie,
Food for gods,
      And my family.

    Grateful for the shining day
Streaming every which way,
      Lighting the very last of May.

    Illness creates a space
To digest, heal, and transform
      Old and new woes.

Digging deep
The well gushes up
    Pure cold water.

Wasp under my eves
Looking for a place
    To make a home.

Two cats eat from same bowl
But must go out
    Through separate doors. Cats.

Children can weary
And gladden the heart,
      So much love blooms.

    Objects decorate
And enhance
      Nests and castles.

    Cities robust and humming
Dot the map and Earth
      With glowing centers.

Why is the sea salty?
Brine and foam,
    Ocean drink strong and wet.

Temperature rising,
Everything is hot,
    Wilting, melting molecules.

Nature's patterns
Grow more intricate
    The closer you look.

The Grand Emptiness
Is only empty
    Of what is false.

    Pure white light
Rushes in to fill the void
    Created by continued effort.

    Old cat, heat-wilted,
Laps some cool water,
    Too exhausted to move.

    Young cat is affronted
By heat,
        Glaringly marshals on.

    Curled dry leaf
Crunches under
        Soft cat pads.

    Drawing is translating
From one dimension to
        Another, and back again.

Color depends on light,
Shadow,
And all adjacent colors.

Even our eyes are subjective,
Seeing and looking,
Do we see? Really?

What makes you, you?
How you look,
Or who looks at you?

Greeting the day
With open arms
    And empty head.

Beauty is so ephemeral,
A rose blooms and fades,
    So our pink health and glow.

Wave goodbye to life,
Temporary stop
    On flight to glory.

 *June*

Warm and delicious,
Days of fun and relaxation,
    Summer is here!

Watermelon days,
Ice cream evenings,
    Marshmallow melting nights.

Snakelike spines,
Vertiginous balance,
    Cats land on four feet.

Climbing higher,
Arriving to look out,
Global wonder awaits.

Vision, hearing,
Touches, tastes,
Tiny fractions of reality.

Bridges over streams
Connecting the divisions
Can also be beautiful.

Runaway thoughts
Distract and confuse.
      Focus necessary.

    Living in the moment
Timelessly experiencing
      Depth of Eternity.

    The narrow range of human
Experience
      Is still wider than we think.

Does it matter that someone
Was here in this life,
    And now they are gone?

Memories fade, faces blur,
Traces dissipate,
    What is left?

Green and growing,
Out my doorway
    Lavish summer garden.

What is here is neglected
By grief sustained.
Letting go is difficult.

Does the Sun go down
Or
Do we go up?

Young cat has first big fight.
Freaked out, but,
Other cat vanquished.

Control does not mean
No feelings, no thoughts;
Control is conscience.

Control is not gripping hard,
Nor squeezing life.
It's breathing understanding.

Youth is taught to control,
Takes a lifetime
To let go and experience.

The body machinery
Works best
        Hydrated, fed, and loved.

    Moving through time
And life,
        One thing remains the same.

    Death peeks out
From behind the
        Invisible curtain.

Amid cacophony of lies,
Love resolves
Life and death.

June bugs,
Creepy crawlies,
Butter, dragon, fireflies.

To capture form, line, color,
Shading and drama
In two dimensions is art.

Symbols contain ancient
Wisdom.
        Deciphering them is genius.

    Ways of thinking
Can help or hinder.
        Seeing them is best.

    Grim reminders
Are stuck unresolved issues,
        Different from realizations.

Great hearts
Are full with gratitude,
    Which spills over to others.

Patience is earned
By transforming agitation
    From oneself and others.

Little bug
Why are you visiting me?
    Too late, cat pounce!

Old cat goes to vet.
Young cat eats mouse.
    Life continues.

    I hang like a drop
At the world's edge,
    Next stop oblivion.

    Birth is a one-way door.
Life is full of doors,
    Death's door is marked EXIT.

Love softens frozen hearts,
Much preferred
    To a tenderizing hammer.

A wonderful meal
Artfully prepared with love,
    Still has to be cleaned up.

Events recur in one's life
Startlingly similar,
    Until we get it right.

Wishing for past happiness
Is a waste of current
    Opportunities.

    Empty your cup,
Soon it will
    Overflow again.

    Battle-gray clouds
Crowding out
    Last patch of blue.

Nature at war with itself
Throws light spears
    And roars through the night.

Homespun wisdom
Is often practical
    And sister of experience.

Strolling through the garden
Of the Master's grounds
    Contemplating beauty.

Wishing is fanciful;
Doing nothing
    To accomplish an aim.

    There is more of me
Than I would like.
    Hard to remember at dinner.

    Pause after the rain,
Soft, clear, and so lovely,
    Such a gentle resolution.

Deep the soul of the Earth
Murmurs a sleepy sound
    And rumbles to turn over.

Bright and sparkly
Remaining drops adorn
    Morning trees and bushes.

All things considered,
The morning after
    Is surprisingly beautiful.

Our great good fortune
Is a constant reminder
To be grateful.

The cusp of Summer,
Golden light streams,
Spring vestiges fade.

Striding bravely forth into
An unknowable future
Leaving worries in the past.

Brown and gold
Pushing out the green,
    Temperature ascends.

Gathering up femininity
Into one cup
    Blushing pink and rose.

More softness,
More firmness,
    Sexes polarize thinking.

New and plump
Baby everythings are adored
Due to cuteness.

Circle of men
Around the wine table,
Predictably imbibing.

Concentrated effort
In a consistent direction
Produces results.

Why struggle and strain
On the stage
    In the theatre of life.

Hangovers are the bane
Of an indulgent
    Night before.

Hearts and minds
Befuddled with age
    Belie suppleness of youth.

Spices, aromatic, exotic
Enhance appetite and senses,
    Plain food fortifies.

    Hunting through the warren
Of life's maze for solutions:
    Look up!

    Your shining face
Lifts my inner life
    On angels' wings.

Love-dipped musings,
Confections wrapped
In lace and harmony.

Sweet are lingering goodbyes,
Sweet are tender reunions,
Sweetest are hearts united.

So fast the days stream by
Like the time machine movie.
Where and when am I?

Laughter in the dark,
Spooky feelings,
   Time to light the candle.

Share a soup and sandwich,
Smiles and happy stories,
   Small things give much joy.

Triple-digit heat wave,
Parboiled air,
   Too hot to draw into lungs.

Coffee; wine glass cradled;
Snowy white tablecloth;
    End of fabulous dinner.

Musicians gather
Attracted to each other,
    Linked molecules.

Shadowless light
Surmounting clarity,
    Etching endless perspective.

Joy shared
With wine paired
    Is joy squared.

    Lopsided cake
Dripping and leaning,
    Unfortunate birthday treat.

    Deep and shallow
Thoughts to challenge,
    Soothe, tease, and amuse.

Cool waters swirling
Over rocks black and wet,
    Replenishing and refreshing.

Small favors add up to
Huge debts,
    Unless love-sponsored.

Immortality, eternal life, sans
The stinging bite of death;
    Light without shadow.

Often is he colored grim,
Searching high and low,
    Looking to find himself.

    Small me, wishing to be
Like high I,
    Only need to disappear.

    Cooking alchemy
Produces aromas
    That melts grumpy moods.

The empty head
Isn't so bad;
The full one, can be worse.

Invisible sizzling energy
Connects those
Marked for higher challenges.

Water witching,
Instinctive mystery,
Practical magic.

Traveling to other places
Affords new perspectives,
    Expansive and renewing.

Familiarity seems safe,
Surroundings invisible:
    A drug-induced illusion.

Leap into an unknown
Environment with eyes open,
    Scared, filled with promise.

Difficult to challenge oneself
Enough to make a difference,
Need outside help to succeed.

Paintings can enlighten,
Giving much pleasure
And color to somber rooms.

New things enter
From the bottom
And rise with the warm air.

Realizing your own position
At any one time
    Is no small thing.

    Living each day accepting
Whatever may come,
    Except for that fly.

    Champagne days,
Dancing molecules,
    Heat-embraced nights.

Being in Rome in a mask,
Immersed in a population
    Of spying art thieves.

Can we modestly receive
Gifts from above
    With gracious appreciation?

Money, a necessary trial,
To count, save, spend,
    Long for, envy, and admire.

The end is in the beginning,
Dissipation in any new idea,
And death in birth.

Real love has no opposite.
Earthly endeavors
Favor duality.

Light and shadow
Play upon the soul,
Stretching depths and heights.

Long thoughts
Reveal history and future
    Of almost everything.

Steaming ground
Coughs up melted rocks,
    Earth is brewing deep below.

Elevated beings carry
The burdens of mere persons
    Lightly in modesty and love.

Angels wear their joy
And compassion
        Gracefully as their halos.

    Skeletal tree, sans leaves,
Touches the rocky ground
        With crooked fingertips.

    Being considerate outranks
Being nice and kind,
        Even outranks affection.

Dry brown earth, burnt black
In patches, fire traces
On tinderbox ground.

Zing! Spirit zips the air –
Sparkling prisms,
Shimmering translucence.

Speeds are subjective,
Heartbeats, breaths, moments,
From gnat to snail to whale.

Praying for rain
Might work
    If you are in a rain forest.

    Liquid evaporating alarmingly,
Surfaces too hot to touch,
    Our star, a glaring red eye.

    Cool evening, glass of wine,
Friends gather together
    Again, with tender affection.

Seamless meetings of
Hearts and minds,
    Sweet energy flowing pink.

Drama finds us when
We are least prepared.
    Defusing hot heads is messy.

Laughter is sweetest,
Light and melodic,
    From a child's heart.

Rain so hard
You can barely walk,
    Dark, wet, and relentless.

Toast and jam,
Simple and effective
    To greet the new day.

    Sowing seeds in a drought
Is heartbreaking;
    And a formula for failure.

It is an uphill struggle
To remain in your body,
In your inner home.

Spiraling skyward Sufi dancer
With outstretched wings,
Going home at last.

Few revelations
Are for everyone,
Ah-Has! tend to be personal.

Modesty becomes any
Who aspire to fame,
        Along with everyone else.

    Strings between mother
And child
        Are stronger than steel.

    A worm in the apple
Can destroy the core,
        Leaving apple unblemished.

Animal parts of us can
Destroy finer sensibilities,
 Leaving beauty untouched.

Grand gestures are
Praiseworthy;
 Thoughtfulness, of more value.

Disarmed by charming
Glances and lowered lashes,
 Feet remain on the ground.

Venice, airy city, barely dry,
Swimming in the
      Mediterranean sunlight.

    Cloudy water,
Image appearing,
      How to interpret the visage?

    Stung by a bee.
Small price to pay,
      Licking honey off fingers.

A growling jet, sky-splitting,
Defiling pure blue,
    Trailing audial pollution.

Lasting impressions
Imprint on eye-backs,
    Beauty, color, etched feelings.

Too much of anything,
Good or bad,
    Can drown judgment.

Some experiences
Take a long time
        To be digested and expelled.

    Rocky shore, wind whipping
Frothy waves, toes wriggling,
        Sandy and cold.

    Where are memories stored?
My body, my heart, my brain?
        All and more, they float above.

Gruesome looking back
At the self who faltered
In the face of difficulties.

Seer is better than the seen,
Remember what triumphs
Past and present hardships.

Worrying produces wrinkles
And bad temperament.
Nothing else.

Product of experiences
Could be wisdom or fear,
        Depending on courage.

    Drape yourself with laurels,
Winning the day,
        Sun shining on your brow.

    Clear blue eyes reflecting
The azure sea
        And love for all beings.

Giggling in the night
At one's own foibles,
    Dramatizing the absurdity.

The many colors of being
Seen in a kaleidoscope;
    Indecipherable non-pattern.

Organization implies
An Organizer,
    Layers of complexity.

Lies, like other crimes,
Betray trusting hearts
      And leave black furrows.

    Traces of fragrance
Lingering in upper rooms
      Hinting at unknown bliss.

    Rooms, locked doors, attics,
Keys to open secrets,
      Not easily acquired.

Peeping over the hedge,
Spying through small window,
Yearning to see an answer.

Dancing in the heart,
Lily stamens flutter,
Waving in – the hapless bee.

Undersea prolific world,
Brilliant hues, myriad forms,
Once again, Nature's ruse.

Dragon breath
Spreading in our foothills,
   Scorching, cleansing all.

Great swaths of ash
Searing lungs and tongues,
   Craving a water drench.

Why question,
When there really is
   Only one true answer?

Clasp your hands
And bow low,
    The maker bestows blessings.

Innermost self of selves
Cries in the dark
    For a hand to reach out.

Graciously accept the
Windfall of your precious life,
    Private and unique.

Dreams can teach, taunt,
Try our patience,
    Or merely entertain the dark.

    Life leaves traces,
Our Earth is crisscrossed
    With layers of time bodies.

    Pouring milk into the gourd,
Kitty lapping,
    Neighbor cat staring.

New growth, quivering green,
Pierces hard clay,
Struggles to reach sunlight.

The blessed rain falls,
Wetting dry, dry ground,
Saving green lives.

Oily, messy life
Oozes on its way
To become fodder.

Taking fragments of meaning
From the miasma of events
      Is heroic work.

    Bubbling wine,
Gentle evening,
      Philosophers meet.

    Black and white,
Opposites contrast, enhance
      Or cancel one another.

Up the mountain pathway,
Steep and rocky at the top.
Don't stop; keep climbing.

Stairway leading up,
Effort to climb,
Easy slide down.

Go, go, go,
Don't stop,
Stopping is death.

Slow motion unfolding rose,
Revealing secret center.
    Petals fall, fragrance remains.

The race from birth to death
Holds twists and turns,
    Many hurdles and surprises.

Usually there is enough
Time or money,
    Usually not both.

What is needed
To complete this moment?
    Seeing that which is here.

The lightest touch
Can move us,
    A heavy hand isn't necessary.

Loving one another
Isn't enough,
    Love the Self in each.

Light is changing,
Shadows lengthen,
　　Evening is swallowing day.

Adversity polishes
Ever-budding patience
　　And blesses the initiate.

Lip to lip,
Heart to heart,
　　Lovers rest in each other.

Hands tracing
Loving faces,
    Fingers interlacing.

Remember the difficult days
When happy, remember
    The pleasant ones when sad.

Proving truth:
A folly.
    Truth stands alone.

View from the top,
Paris all around,
        Nothing is more sublime.

    What is happening?
Everything changes,
        No holds to slow transitions.

    Walking between timelines,
Viewing static Eternity,
        Wondering about beginnings.

Passions fade with
Blunted ambition and
    Abandoned dreams.

Kindness comes
Not from weakness,
    But from awareness of reality.

Most precious treasure
Is hidden
    Lest it become ubiquitous.

Honor, altruism, camaraderie,
It is possible to be more
    Than is usually aspired to.

    Envy, jealousy, enmity
Are ways to torture oneself,
    Defiling chances for love.

    When life's tapestry
Is brutally cut
    Grieving is no joke.

Peak of Summer
Sweeping through canyons,
  Melting rivers into steam.

Taking the time it takes
To accomplish each task;
  Not fretting, but cherishing.

Ever rushing to get nowhere
As fast as one possibly can,
  Arriving without one's Self.

Sainthood isn't for everyone,
Remember to forgive yourself,
      Guilt is maybe the worst sin.

    To remember Winter's cool
In Summer's heat,
      Helps to stay on even ground.

    Plunging into the lake,
Flipping over to view the stars,
      Floating cool galaxy member.

Shine from all those suns,
Still, space is a dark place;
This universe needs our light.

July

    First light
A hush
        Birds begin.

    Life's drama, we the actors,
Maybe meet the director,
        Never meet the author.

    Friendship, family, closeness
Between people,
        Provides opportunities to care.

Last light,
Stars appear,
   Crickets begin.

Stars and stripes forever,
Fireworks blooming,
   American freedom nostalgia.

True remedy
For many troubles
   Is prioritizing.

Great eye of the sky
Ennoble your bathers,
    But not with sunburn.

    That which is obvious
Can be obscure:
    Remove your blinders.

    Steppingstones leading
To the temple retreat,
    Narrow gate beckoning.

Dust of the world
Shaken from my feet,
    Ready to rise cleanly.

Purity of soul
Squandered
    On unholy junk jewelry.

Nature's complexity
Fits together harmoniously
    Like no human-made puzzle.

Retaining inner focus
On what feeds spirit
Helps to see wrong turns.

Educating requires
Sharing
Our best understandings.

Learning requires
Accepting
We don't know everything.

Loved ones can show us
Our flaws
If we let them.

No one owes you happiness,
It is purchased
Through your own efforts.

I would like a dress of water
To slosh around,
Always clean, always fresh.

White horse on hilltop
Surveys
        Valley below.

    Eucalyptus trees,
Leaves fluttering in breeze,
        Aroma envelops.

    Share every ounce
Of the best in you,
        Someone else will join in.

The Sun shares its glory
With our world, even
    The Moon's beauty is borrowed.

Lying in the sand
Salty water tickling toes,
    Tiny crabs scuttle over me.

No external enemy
Can do to us
    What our own inner voices do.

Divine inspiration
Can visit in a quiet moment,
   Transforming priorities.

The flutter of angels' wings,
The softest melody,
   Can penetrate our defenses.

True nobility
Pierces heart,
   Lays down life for love.

We claim to be many things,
Yet events transpire
Revealing our pretense.

Digging for hidden treasure
Won't make you rich,
But might make you happy.

Confusion is a glitch
In seamless sleep,
A chance to actually decide.

Shining body of light
Moves through the living air
      Invisibly penetrating solids.

    Love unites the circle
Of past and future
      In the ever perfect Present.

www.ingramcontent.com/pod-product-compliance
Lightning Source LLC
Chambersburg PA
CBHW031415290426
44110CB00011B/391